# THE MUSIC OF HANDS

*Theresa Senato Edwards*

The Music of Hands: Poems
Copyright © 2012 by Theresa Senato Edwards

Cover art Copyright © 2012 by Christine Ashton
Used with permission. Artist's website: www.blu282.com.

Author photograph Copyright © 2012 by Douglas Edwards.
Used with permission.

Cover design by Theresa Senato Edwards.

All rights reserved. No part of this publication may be reproduced or transmitted in any form or by any means, electronic or mechanical, without permission in writing from the author, except by reviewers who may quote brief excerpts in connection with a review in a newspaper, magazine, or electronic publication. Requests for permission to make copies of any part of this work should be e-mailed to the author; her email can be found on her blog: TACSE *creations*, www.tacse.blogspot.com.

Published in the United States by Theresa Senato Edwards, Poughkeepsie, New York.

ISBN: 13: 978-1480211469
ISBN-10: 148021146X

~

First edition, November 2012

*giving thanks ...*

# CONTENTS

Uterus 9
What the Fingers Remember 10
Holly Rose 11
Architecture 13
Afternoon 14
As I think of ways to pray 15
What's Not Broken 16
Around the First 17
The Music of Your Hands 18

Glove making 23
Monochrome man 24
On Shadows 25
Creature Elegy 26
The Sorrow of Swans 27
Juncture 29
brother carried the poppies 30
death: 31
The Music of Dead Hands 32

Acknowledgements 35
About the Author 35

*and the dead scattered to the four corners of their bodies
were mended by women's hands*

~ Venus Khoury-Ghata, "Early Childhood"
    Translated by Marilyn Hacker

**Uterus**

At 51, I can live without you, weathered pear,
matched muscle of my sisters, like mother's body.

In the time it takes to pray, you're sliced in strips
like butter. Hollow sound interrupted, a faint
sorrow as if an elegy's only passing was from
one woman's hand to another.

I really wasn't aware of your significance or what
you were the last 16 years: dark vessel, mother
loneliness. I wasn't tested for clarity. The pressing
under skin phantom now.   I know your worth.

## What the Fingers Remember

At first, nothing

tap / but words rely on sight,
peripheral vision,
stroking precise
anticipated—
indexes trot, slowly dance
the cha cha with eyes.

After practice, precision

fingers placed to promenade
lettered bleachers,
beveled feel of display—
eyes down
then balance: square, air,
square, air, square air.

After routine, language

knowing the dance routine
without eyes—
as if touch were sight,
a soft brail stippled
in the brain, like love, the
surreal of senses / like learning.

*after reading Christine Klocek-Lim's chapbook*
*Ballroom: a love story*

## Holly Rose

Her eyes listen to the tattoo artist—
a dance of curls beneath a winter hat
he wears inside his parlor.
Joker tattoo on his forearm,
ear lobes half moons of studs.

All of a sudden, her ears—
snap of sterile gloves, metal overcomes
air as he tests his machine, then applies
the pattern for her third tattoo.

Pain outlines her stomach left of the
belly button. Blackened rip of body made
by covered hands that guide the tool's
cut, then wipe her blood into the past.
Stale space sucks color from her face,
carves symbols of her parents.

His lean legs straddle the chair's side;
she imagines them against her, tries to grab
leather before her lover's thick, strong body
situates in her mind. Below her ribs vine
and stem fuse in remembrance: holly for
December (her father's birthday month),
rose for June (her mother's).

Their inked tribute lost momentarily in obsession:
artist's art, new genus on skin.

~

She goes back for color;
goes back for him,
This time lidocaine two hours before
helps numb the needle's entry.

His winter hat with "FUCK YOU"
on the back. Clean gloves pour
ink in tiny, sterile plastic. She
follows his blue eyes, his grey
chin hairs stroked in her mind.

"Came in three hours ago,
turned the heat on for you," he says.
She's hot below her inked flower,
her lover's touch the night before.
She laughs, drone shades skin
until the lidocaine wears off.

He asks if it hurts. *Excruciating*,
she thinks. "This is it for me." she says.
"Last time in this place." He rattles her,
loudly snaps latex from his hands,
says, "Maybe I'll see ya not for a tattoo."
Her lover's trust between her thighs.
Parents' love, reminder of loyalty
she'll wear with chance of only fading.

She listens—
leaves the noise behind.

**Architecture**

The folds in her hands, church pamphlets, every figment set in the old balcony's smell, her father's smell when he sleeps too long in the back bedroom, back to the opening which begins stairs, those folds of wood grinding time down to nonexistence, pointed structure gone from wind, dirty bed sheets folded like prayers.

*riff on "fold" from Laura McCullough's poem "Longing"*

**Afternoon**
    *for Ingrid*

I pray for bone
    the growing of it
visualize   sticky   chewing gum
    on my hands to wrap
around leftovers, fragments tiring
    looking for their other halves
I delicately pull   your spine hollow light
    grasp both ends   fuse,
my fingertips moan.

**As I think of ways to pray**

I want to linger, touch doorknobs
again,     prayer smoothes the turning
because knobs have teeth, knobs are open
mouths that withstand repetitions.  If only
I learned how to say the rosary, like a saint
affixed to a story, smoothing my fingers on
each bead.  Did I say knobs have teeth?  Did I say
each bead was repetitive?  It's the safest way to
pray without thinking too much.  It's the best
way to pray during radiation treatment: steady
with sincere asking.  "Offer up!" is what
my friend said.  Her brother's a priest.

> *riff on "I want to linger, touch doorknobs" from
> Bryan Borland's poem "The Day I Pack His Things"*

**What's Not Broken**

The promise you made to your mother. The black urn
molded around your father's bones. Your hands

when you smooth the blanket at the bed's edge.
Neatly tucked corners. Winter's white line along

the roof. Marriage vows after nineteen years. Unbroken,
the silent tempo of time. Eighty-year-old front porch

screens. That old green house you love so much. Kitten's
fixed leg—before, a limp wave of fur. Unbroken,

a victim's shriek that carries the night. Last June's
steady stream to the river. Street light at driveway's

end. Kindness from a long-time friend. Unbroken
tubes of blood in my hands. The young oncologist's

voice. A black sky I fall into. What has been steady,
level, relentless all these years? The nun's

ruler on my knuckles. Rules. Age lines around
my eyes. A good mother's love. Imagine, suppose,

consider magic spells, the way rain rocks you steady
to sleep. That continuous sea in my brain, dark red paper

cleverly folded like a heart.

*after reading "What's Broken" by Dorianne Laux*

**Around the First**

Attic room: unmade twin beds
old, dirty casement windows
needing curtains to hide
the way he broke inside her silence.

Old, dirty casement windows
cracked from the rain within:
the way he broke inside her silence.
Ceiling, pitched and peeling

cracked from the rain within,
low and suffocating.
Ceiling, pitched and peeling,
the smell of skin

low and suffocating
in thick teenage air.
The smell of skin
lit the lamp.

## The Music of Your Hands
> *at the very heart of bully prevention is the need for individuals to become "special."* ~ J. Richard Knapp

the music of your hands

*follows*
        invisible roads,
fleshy snags droop but hold the octaves
just outside your worry world
        you've hidden, upturned mouth,
fingers fuse, an interval of wanting, narrow
glass wall you're hesitant to explore

the music of your hands

*cushions*
        your sound,
preparing for a motif, soft careening
dissonance needing more
        you've hidden, aching temples,
fingertips sore from the rubbing
in your brain

the music of your hands

*refuses*
        their scorn,
a special quiet carries,
        you've shared the melody, monotone
then rising,
your palms understand    clear a meshing
of indifference.

*Cold worlds shake from the oar.*
*The spirit of blackness is in us, it is in the fishes.*
*A snag is lifting a valedictory, pale hand;*

~ Sylvia Plath, "Crossing the Water"

**Glove making**

Trace time, skin    hand pattern.
Thumb for loneliness like yesterday's wind.
Table wings cut carefully, lie listless, waiting for life.
Gussets: the in-betweens made of cold, blue upholstery.
My thumb/index finger stretch to push through tin:
mother's tiny element.    Black thread.
Rain outside pushes me to pins.
Blue upholstery cut for one promise: cover her dead knuckles.
Unmatched buttons beneath round, rusted seal, one
for each strand of DNA.
Stitch slowly    sorry for death to new things.

**Monochrome man**

hugged my mother once at the bottom of stairs in between doorway and hall. She didn't see his gentle pressing.

I see him through thick time. When my son was three, he bled. Blood-blister in his throat emptied red threads onto sheets. Man's sheer sleeve absorbs. When my son was four, the babysitter spoke little English, watched too many children. End of hall, babies cried in a room stuffed with brown, wooden cribs. Clear plastic couches in her living room. Toddler gate my son pounded each morning; man tends to his ache. In kindergarten my son learned Spanish but couldn't make letters on pages stay still. Man catches little-boy vowels in his collar, helps consonants dissolve: black salt in thick, pale hands press together lightly, fingertips pointing.

In the shower I cried, water pelting my chest, colorless, shapeless, molding into monochrome, the indefinite pulling me away. Man folds me along the edges, like fresh linen mother placed in dresser drawers; his soft eyes urge me beyond the weight.

**On Shadows**

a tree cracks below its wishbone limbs
where houses begin their illusionary
descent toward the untouchable:
gaping darkness off refracted structures

where black specks on blue home
seep through until all that's left
is sponge

where chalk-white windows
teach in retrospect: "remember,
don't talk to strangers"

where mother tree rootless,
clueless, larger than sun,
poses for blue sky

green grass alligator—
nowhere to run except on shadows

*in response to Ann Calandro's collage, Shadows*

**Creature Elegy**

I'm tired of killing them, naked
widows foraging for dark space,

hanging from cloth, translucence
strong as life. Blood legs dart

from giant death—grim perspective.
The attic swells to hold them in,

long legs, fine threads between my
fingers. Heads covered, crushed in

tissue—black rouge. Venom, my
scrutiny: human subtraction, one

limb then another. Shear bulbous
babies soften before death.

**The Sorrow of Swans**
> *I have looked upon those brilliant creatures,*
> *And now my heart is sore.* ~ William Butler Yeats

And if I were to answer,
describe a little boy with swans
who felt the lining of their hearts,
shoreline of sadness,
I would applaud his father's
hands pulling frozen belly
from a feathered hump
of snow on concrete.

If I had looked away,
modern home, windows thick
with light, I might have saved
my own sorrow. Little boy,
their gallant witness to nature's
murderers: water rats surround
new life, misty greys that flutter
feathers not nearly ready to be wings.

And swans break   wail danger.
Cygnets snatched beneath a murky lake,
a bright survival enemies demand. If I
had not begun to count the distant greys,
maybe white, quill curves in water
would provoke in me more joy.

But I remember his voice, high pitched
to carve away frailties: when swans
orchestrated air but could not save them
all. And my boy accepted this, brought
bread, names for each babe left. If I did not
watch this collaboration, ripples of absence,
I might have yearned for swans like Yeats.

If I were to answer, describe a little boy
with swans, I would hope for life found
through dreams. I might have seen dead
hands, white as ice, lay themselves upon
a heap, bring it back to him. Instead, last swan
makes a frozen path along concrete, nearing
our door it never reaches. Snow high behind
a dumpster, backdrop to what my husband
knows he'll feel come morning: an icy, prickled
neck to pry its body from an empty    early air.

**Juncture**

Reach beyond the ribs,
close to heartbreak, smooth
the fire in the sockets,
weld fingertips to trees.

Talk to chalky clouds, clench
the strand of night tied to your jaw,
as if skeleton were prayer music.

**brother carried the poppies**
*for donavon*

brother carried the poppies,
said, "it isn't enough
to touch the valleys of your heart,
I need to scrape the linings
of your valley, I need to breathe in
the blues of your lungs
until I turn yellow"

I sat fogged-over,
caves sculpted beneath
my eyes.

~

I walked behind,
brother carried the poppies,
said, "it isn't enough to stroke
your tree wild from drought,
suck the lily white,
I need to press your valley hard,
then run silent, a cat through snow"

I said, "the lake hits hard,
your body pounding,
its sting I'll taste regardless."

**death:**

the journey of swell waves ~
in a husband's arms,    smooth
darkness to wind
a shedding, grit from a low place.
rising crucial
a look at decay
expanse.
foldingrollingfoldingrollingfoldingrollingfoldingrolling
the surge of birds' wings
holding
~ just holding.
god tows    rifts,
sound    absorbs.

## The Music of Dead Hands

*rests*
      silent overtones of the past cushion the fingers
huddled like fleshy sticks ready for a bonfire
or maybe the earth: a dark, wet baritone.

You wait for a beat, slight hint of flux,
what syncopated memories feel like against white cloth,
pristine maple edges,
      the force of thought:
what limbs are before arteries fill
with disinfectant.

*repeats*
      the similar alignment of muddy wrists,
a likeness among death in coffins,
hands in unison just below the waist
or maybe a leitmotif: calm persona
amid parallels of grief.

You wait for a variation, faint twist of harmony
from knuckles muffled in wood or steel:
unfinished symphonies,
      what ache sounds like.

*resolves*
      a room full of dead hands in hydrogel,
fingertips stiff amid indefiniteness.

You peer through the large glass wall,
wait for the air's rush and pitch,
      or maybe applause: strong dance of palms,
a rippling dissonance,
then suspension: a final holding
of clay, the mind's last form of whole,
      each hand a slow, waving cadence.

## ACKNOWLEDGEMENTS

Grateful acknowledgement is made to the editors of the following literary journals in which the following poems or earlier versions of them first appeared and/or were republished:

*13 Myna birds*: "On Shadows"
*Blue Earth Review*: "What's Not Broken"
*Caper Literary Journal*: "The Music of Dead Hands" and "Monochrome man"
*Coldfront Magazine*: "Glove making" featured link in *this morning* on August 4, 2012
*International Bully Prevention E-zine*: "The Music of Your Hands"
*The Journal of Compressed Creative Arts*—Matter Press: "Juncture"
*Referential*: "Architecture" and "As I think of ways to pray"
*Seven CirclePress*: "Holly Rose"
*Thrush*: "Glove making"
*Whale Sound*: "Monochrome man" republished with audio

Thanks always to Doug, Richard, and Troy.

~

## ABOUT THE AUTHOR

Theresa Senato Edwards' first book of poems, *Voices Through Skin*, was published June 2011 by Sibling Rivalry Press. A poem from this book entitled "Her Rituals" was a poetry finalist for the 2011 OCD Foundation's Dare to Believe Contest.

Her second book, *Painting Czeslawa Kwoka ~ Honoring Children of the Holocaust*, a full-color collaboration with Painter, Lori Schreiner, was published by unbound CONTENT, April 2012. The title piece, "Painting Czeslawa Kwoka," won the Tacenda Literary Award for Best Collaboration 2007; another piece in the collaboration, "A Last Look," won this same award in 2010; and the collection won the Tacenda Literary Award for Best Book, 2011—all awards from BleakHouse Publishing.

Theresa's blog: TACSE *creations*: www.tacse.blogspot.com.

Made in the USA
Charleston, SC
25 November 2013